BEFORE IT'S TOO LATE

FARHAN MHMD

"All thanks to her, Even though I have no role in her life, but one day I will be the most important person in her life."

Contents

PREFACE

"**"At some point in life , someone will love you more that what you've expected. Be patient and learn to wait because sometimes, a patients person receives the best love story."**

This book is all about a young man, who met his love of his life and the sacrifices that he have done to show that how much he loved her. Until she realized him it was too late, she was helpless and even him, both wanted their life togather but at the time changes everything. Its not quite simple to achive every dream to come true, when we are in love with someone. In the same way the time made them apart and both leads their own life.This book includes both my experience and my imagination. some love story ends with happiness and some other with tragic ending."

when we me met.

It was a busy day after all my exams, its was time for me to go back home. wow! the word home sounds so sweet, when you go out and start a new life. home is the place where youu will have food cooked by your mother,you own atmoshpere that your born and brought up, only those things were inside my mind.I packed my bag and moved to the bus stop,after an hour the bus had arrived and I got into it. Always i would be standing my half journey,because of the crowd that was the worst part my journey.But this time I was lucky that one seat was left.I ran over there and sat there before someone else would find it out. And there was young man seated near me, turning his face towards the window.I wanted to sit there near the window.I so tapped him to ask can I sit there, he turned to me, his eyes was filled with tears, when I saw him I came to know that he was passing through something. when I saw that I said "its okay you sit there". He did utter a word just got up from there and gestured me to have the seat there. I felt guilt of asking him that seat. I wanted to speak to him but I don't know how to start a conversation. I saw him looking at a something in his mobile and his tear drops that had fallen in it, I asked him "are you alright",he just gave me a smile,wipeing up his tears ."Yeah, Iam good". There was something that's hunting him down, and I wanted to know what he was going through. but I can't ask him directly, so i started to talk to him,"hi i am farhan",waved our hands "hello, I am shahid".

Farhan- where are you going ?

Shahid- up to mysore .

Farhan- home.

Shahid- nop! to attande the marriage.

Farhan- oh! what are you doing ?

Shahid- I am an medicine student.

Farhan-oh great.

after that he muted and again started stareing at the mobile again. I asked him if you don't mind asking Isaw you looking this picture and your eyes filled with tears, what is that about?. he gave me a smile and showed me, it was a wedding invitation, written Mujeeb *weds safa*". I asked him is it your girlfriend, how did you guys brokeup. "No she is not my girlfriend,neither we broke up". Then what happend why are you looking so upset after seeing it. it's a long story brother. I don't care how long the story is, I just need to hear his story and waste my time until I reach my hometown.

HIS STORY

I was from a middle class family, dad had kept many hopes and my graduation day was my mom's dream .With all this hopes of making my parents proud and also with a good score sheet I got admitted into the medical college of Calicut. At last the campus days starts with all the boring lectures and some seminars.it was my first time staying away from my home so long, I had my batchmate has my room mates, so making friends became easier than I thought. finally the regular classes stared. The new faces and huge classrooms where many dreams were flowing like water, some came there for just to enjoy there campus life, some with their parents force and some others to achieve something ,still today I did not understand, why am I there for. we boys have a special skills of focusing on girls and same way these girls way some extraordinary skills of looking over boys without their notice, As usually I was also focusing on girls, Until I met her, a pointed nosed girl,worn a black kurthaand cover her hair with a red shawl going through the corridor, I was not beliving in the love at first sight but when I saw her I just felt it. I was egarly waiting to know who is she? . later during the class some one opened the door entered, oh my god it was her, I was very happy to know that she is not my senior rather she is classmate.I wanted to know her name but I was not brave enough to ask her. Meanwhile ,one off my friend noticed my abnormal behavior went near her and asked her what's your name ,i was waiting for that movement to listen her sweet voice ,she said i am ***safa.*** After listening to this my mind told me to hug and give big kiss to my friend ***shah***, who asked her name ,after that he came near me and asked how are u feeling now and my reply was an hug no him ,he said don't thank me , rather buy me a tea and snacks for helping you, whatever it may be it was a great help he did .All needed to creat a friendship with her,so started speaking with her. At the beginning I started approaching her with some douts on subjects later I collected her number and started messaging her.

She is very focused on her studies ,born and brought up at London with all these short information i stared building conversation and later created a friendship bond and she had very cool nature and straight forward behavior and that made my love even more towards her. Our bond slowly started growing more strong she was a bright student, spending days with her, I did not understand, that how fast that one year had passed, we had already done with our first semester and the second semester exam was already near. I wanted to say her that i love her but I was afraid that it may affect our friendship and if i say it now, will it effect to her studies. I stayed clam because for me her dream was more valuable than my life. we use to have long night conversation started with asking her some doubt now texting her became an daily routine, her family was financially sounded and her father have hospitals at London and she used to go home every weekends to Mysore, one of her main passion is driving, she drives crazy when she is on wheels . After our whole exams got over, it was vacation for 2 months long everyone including her was happy, first time in my life i was not happy with these vacation because one thing that i would miss her so badly ,she usually goes to her dad when there is 3 to 4 days of holidays and without fail she use to bring me the chocolates at any cost. After we came back from the examination hall, we were discussing the question paper after all discussions were over she asked me "what's yours holiday plan" ,inside me it was like I hate this holiday and i want you stay along with me ,she waved the hand in front of my face and asked me where in world are you and simply nodded my head and said I have and football match tomorrow, later on I am moving back to my home .what's your plan i asked she looked up and said going meet my dad and spend time with him and smiled. her driver had already waiting for her Infront of a black GLC black mated Benz ,that looked hot .when she saw him arrived she waved me and got into the car . after some couple of hours she had sent a text message had she have reached home and i was busy with team meeting and when i saw the message it was already 2 at night and replies with an smiling emoji but she had already asleep ,later next day it was matchday and she had seen my message and sent me an good Moring with an all the best to your todays match , i was so happy to see this message and latterly i already won the match there ,after her reading the text .

bus had parked near an hotel for a tea break, has ask me shall we have a coffee, I said yes and we both got down and ordered a coffee he took a cigarette out of his pocket and offered me one i nodded that i wont smoke ,so he lit it and took a puff and slowly released it ,i asked him why do you smoke ,before telling anything he used give me a smile and he continued.......

i was an chain smoker and if you ask me why do you smoke it's an another story. oh *my god this guy have many story and he stared saying it .* some people enter into our life and leave but they always keep some memories that hunts us down. i had another relationship earlier when i was in 11th std it was her gift, after we broke up. i got a new habit of smoking to forget her. i was very upset when she left and my some of my friends used to smoke and when i went to them after we broke up ,they were smoking and when they saw me in dull and anger mood asked me what happened ,i narrated the whole story and when i said about our breakup they stared laughing at me ,i stayed quite and they said me that let her go ,we will find a new one ,or lets try on her sister ,these friends are so much bunch of dogs made laugh even in my sad condition, they started smoking and looked at me and asked why are you standing here ,get lost don't kill yourself by taking the 60% and i was confused what? what 60% ,then he said when someone smokes he takes 40% of smoke inside and let other 60% outside so get-out from here , I asked him can i borrow one ,he asked me what ? cigarette ,he looked at me and are you out of your nuts or did she hit you on your head , my friends used to smoke but they never support a new smoker or anyone to smoke ,now i came to know why they have warned me to not to smoke, i refused them and took a cigarette from it and lighted it , i took a long smoke from it and released it in the same way ,oh my god in heaven ,i started coughing like any think and they started laughing like any think slowly i started learning how to smoke and at the beginning i used to smoke more than a pack .at first it was for just an relaxation but now it became a part of my life and now i am trying to quit it ,for her, my *Lana.* stared because of a girl now quitting it for a girl.

we finished our coffee and he finished lighting up two cigarettes ,and slowly moved into the bus .and asked him what happened after you read her message , he took a deep breath and ......

"shahid its time we go " ,shah shouted, i took a cigarette started smoking it with the happy face and we moved on to the collage ground ,it was an interclass competition and we were the freshers batch ,our team had good players and we were playing with our direct senior batch that was 2nd years and it was 3-2 in the score board when it was full time , i had scored one goal and we won with 1 goal ahead. later on we had matches with 4th years and 3rd years had already moved into finals it was a very good match and had a tough competition .The score board was with 1-1 both the team was in pressure and the referee blew the whistle , it was an penalty shootout and an red card for our seniors, it was our only hope to win this match ,meanwhile it started raining and the management told us to finish this match and the finals will be help tomorrow ,bipin our team captain insisted me to have the shot and i was waiting for that . the keeper came near me and splinted his chewing gum on the field and an arrogant look ,the referee blew up i took a shot run and hit the ball towards left side corner and the keeper had jumped to right side .it was goal... everyone on the bench started cheering us and after 5 minutes the score board was 2-1 and we won the match after our celebration of getting into finals ,i messaged her about our win and getting into finals ,she was happy. Later on i rode back to room with my bike , on way to my hostel i met with an accident and has badly wounded everyone surrounded and took me to the hospital ,after two days of i got my conscious back and already had done with two surgeries and my vacation was now at bed .when she came to know about this there was 20 missed call in my phone ,i called her back when i saw that ,that was the first time we spoke on phone and that call lasted for about half an hour .that day i realized that she was very caring and she shouted at me for not wearing helmet. her words always provoked me .i thought she had a same feeling what i have towards her .after some days in our conversation i proposed her ... "*Lana , we have shared mostly an year together. each and every day we talk to each other and share for feelings even its good or bad ,we find solution to each other , from the day i saw you i had fell in love with you . at the begging i thought i would forget you but day by day when our bond became thicker ,my love towards you started growing more and more often ,i can promise you that i would give more happiness then sorrow . we build a great future together ,all i need a yes word from you, and whatever it may be your reply ,promise me that you it will not effect our friendship ,take your own time to think* "i had already red this for 4 to 5 times before sending it and later i sent this message ,my heart beat was so fast and each and sound near me was very much adorable for me . it had been 3 minutes after i had sent her ,she have seen that and she was offline and i was fallen asleep ..when i woke up in the morning i saw the notification from her ,i quickly open my screen and its her message in the top , open her massage and started reading it ,for all the essay format of my message she gave me a reply in a single word "*I AM NOT INTRESTED*" that message hopefully broke me and sent her "*please promise me that you will talk to me and it will not effect our friendship*" she had seen this and replied me that" i am not sure ,it depends " uff! this message had almost torn me apart. and she went offline .all my pain mixed into one ,i was not even able to show my face to her. i was completely lost ,don't know what to do ,what to say ,later she haven't sent a single message or an call from her .she completely ignored me .the friendship we built from an year was completely destroyed in just seconds.

After our vacation i came back to class everyone was asking me how are you and what happened ,she had not even talked to me but she never looked at me .In my mind it was blending that why the hell did i come ,its better i could have stayed home ,if i think of going to talk to her ,i was not bold enough to face her after creating such a mess .what ever it may be i had an hope of that i could fix this .slowly again i started messaging her ,but this time she had kept more distance from me ,one day when i brought a new mobile ,my friends asked me throw a party and she was in them but she was not knowing about it, i brought them to our canteen they all ordered the ice-cream and when i had to pay the bill i did not have enough money and said him that i would pay him evening and said ok ,she had noticed it and when we reached the class she came near me and gave the money ,i asked her why was she giving me ,she said that she don't like owing from others ,that word others had almost hit me to death ,and i was helpless for that but i did not take money from her instead i said that this my party and nobody pays for the party of others and i refused to take that money from her .

later she asked my friends if could take that money from her she would offer them a treat ,my dear friends came to me said about this when they came know about this they refused to have the treat and said her give the money by herself. later i used message her sometimes and one day i asked her that does my message irritate you she replied me that she don't like texting that's all . and she was this to me ,once who was texting the whole night me and now she don't like texting . my roommate noticed that my smoking was been increasing day by day and they came to know the reason ,they started advising me ,but my love for her is growing day by day .i used call her with my friends mobile and made them to talk to just hear her voice , an whole year passed in this way and it was our 3rd year ,juniors had come ,shah was focusing on a girl and got committed in 2 months with that girl all where telling me to get committed with someone else so that you would forget her ,but loveing her inside i could not pretend or fake love someone because i know how much that hhurts when your partner comes to know about it ,so i dont want to do that .

But now a days she used to look at me and smile at me ,and all that looks and smile was far enough for me rather than her ingnorence , later there held a camp in an tribel area for our batch any each camp tent consited of two members each .as i wished it happend we both were on same team and thanks to DR.muzamil for makeing us in one team because he was leading the camp and he knew my whole story ,he came to me and this your last chance just make it work out because there only one year left ,he was my classmate and roommate and he was much worried about my smoking and I had promised him I would quit it soon and he create this chance so that I would quit and on Sunday evening we reached in that tribble village and it was a 10 days camp and we were staying in tented . a good Monday morning I woke early in the morning dressed up and went the camp ,when I was already there was in the camp I was the first person to reach there .I was already working on project ,that Muzammil had told me about a project that Lana was working which her father had assigned her to do for their hospital and she had promised him that she would do that ,but she was trying hard to finish it by time and she wouldn't do it ,so I thought I would do that for her and give her a surprise ,from last 3 days I was working on that ,even I have worked so much hard for my own collage project . has I reached earlier in camp I open my lap and started working on that ,I did not notice she had arrived there .she came and sat near me and asked me what are you doing .i said working on a project and she asked me that she would help me but i refused that and told her that's fine i can handle it ,after few hours ,seeing my workload she asked me again that she can help me if i want ,but again i refused and said her to take rest .she opened her bag and took the water bottle ,it was so sunny day that i was my whole body was sweating ,she offered me a cup of cold water and said me drink the water and later work on the project .i looked at her and took water and started drinking it and her phone beeps and it was her dad ,she received it and moved from there ,after that she came to the camp and she started working on the same project that i was working for her ,she was been working it from past 10 days and today was the last date and she was not done with it yet . at last I finished that project .her phone beeps again and it was her dad she answered it and she was saying that I almost finished it ,after hanging up she was murmuring herself and working on it , shah called her for some work and she went with him I had finished the whole project and checked it again already crowd had been coming for the program . I created a fake email and mailed her. She came back and open her laptop and saw a notification ,she opened it and it was her project from and it was from an unknown mail ,she was shocked and was very happy for it and called Muzammil asking that have he sent any mail he said that he have not sent anything .she was in a happy mood and sent that mail to her dad and called him ."*I have sent it just check it and say me whether is it okay or should I change anything* " and hanged her phone .she was talking like the whole project was her own idea .i was just looking at the patients but my whole concentration has on her .she came near me stared helping me with my work ,I asked her what happened you are in good mood .yeah! didn't I tell you about the work I completed it and sent it to my dad and he was so happy with it ,thank god ,she told turned towards the patients I asked her you told me that It wasn't over yet , no I just finished it .me who knows the whole truth about that project and first of all it was me one who done the whole project and she did not reveal the truth .later it was evening we finished the camp and headed back to our tents .i was so tiered that I would go asleep on busy street .but I to had explore the village ,I took a bath from the near by pond and dressed up and went outside .i was fond the village atmosphere that climate .i open my phone I had 2 missed call from my mother .i called her back ,these mothers are so different from whole world because they how much you grow older you are still any small child for them and they take care of each and everything and their children are only their priority even he or she is married they don't allow anyone in their position . she picked up the call and asked me about what you are doing, how are you, did you have coffee and how is the climate there, did you apply the oil on your hair etc....... she asked everything and told me go to bed fast and hanged up. I came near tea stall and ordered a tea and brought a cigarette and I lighted it opened the social media I was smoking a drinking the tea." hey shahid " I hear a voice I looked around and I did not find any one ,later someone tapped me from behind ,when turned back it was her Lana, the smoke inside my mouth came out and started coughing ,she moved back because of that smoke and started scolding me .

Lana - "from when did this habit came to you, why do you pay money to die, give that some poor that may give some good deeds ", listening that I throwed that cigarette, it was my first time I threw the cigarette without finishing it ,it was only because she had been there and I don't want to create a bad impression ,

Shahid- "sorry ,madam .yeah tell me why did you come to see me ".

she sat near me

Lana- "I had been to Muzammil ,tell me the truth was it you who sent me the mail ",

I nodded and said

Shahid- "no it wasn't me and what is this mail about",

she stared at me

Lana- "don't act to much, tell me the truth or else wait let me call Muzammil".

Shahid- "no that's fine, yeah it was me, Muzammil had told about your project and you not able complete it ,so I thought I could help you"

Lana-" okay and why didn't you tell me about it, In the morning"

Shahid- "I don't like owing things from others so ,I did mention you about it "

Lana- "by the way thanks"

Shahid – "your welcome"

Lana – "don't start smoking again, I am leaving"

Shahid – "don't leave, always be with me than I won't smoke again"

Looking at me and laughing she nodded and headed back to her tent. i was just laughing by thinking her words and happier that she cares about me. I think I got my old Lana back even though she knows that I love her. After the dinner went back to the tent, I had a good sleep. i got up late that day and already everyone had been there at work. she had been there before I reach there, she was looking more beautiful than before, I don't know is it because my love towards her had grown more or she is always like that. she waved at me, and we stared helping each other we enjoyed our camp ,it was time for lunch and I just called her that lets have the lunch together and she said okay fine then let's go , we went an hotel inside that village and had the lunch there it was very wonderful to spend time with her ,her voice and her naughty attitude and always that pointed nose that was the first thing I noticed ,when she came into the class at the beginning later having the lunch we moved into the camp one way she asked me do you still love me ,I did not reply anything.

Okay fine don't tell me.my inner voice was shouting like "how can I tell you, how much I love you, don't act has a fool, knowing everything" but my voice did not come out, we just walked silently. Days passed so fast, and I got my Lana back with this camp. she used to go have the food together, visiting the village .no day while crossing the road she holds my hands and l looked at her, but she wasn't looking at me, I started shivering with fear. We almost walked miles together holding our hands, finally we reached back to our tents it was last day of our camp she looked at me, we both met with an eye contact and stayed a long time like that. all she wanted to say was in her eye and I think she really loved me, but she never told me that she loved me. later that night I lost my whole sleep I was just thinking of that, my eyes started rolling the tears, I would not control my emotions, I started crying like child. I was not able to sleep that whole night, next day morning she came in search of, it was an early morning I was near the lake side, I was so sleepy, and she came near me and asked me why you are standing here, I said, just like that enjoying the view. why are you crying? she asked me. I am not crying; I did not sleep the whole night yesterday. I thought she would ask me why? but she did not because she knew the reason. we sat there for long time ,slowly I kept my head on her shoulder ,she did not react for it instead she made it more comfortable for me. After an hour her phone rang and it was her friend and she had go, she asked me when are you leaving I said later . I was not ready to leave that place because that place had given me more memories of her, that's the place where spent our most important part of my life ,and that place will always be special one for me . she packed her bag and everyone started moving into the bus I had already packed my bag ,I went to bus at sat near the window .Muzammil who saw me gave me a smile like he couldn't help me more than this .and I was very thankful for him. That day at night we reached back to our hostel. I slept as I went into the bed .after two days of rest and holiday we came back to class and I was looking for her, she was not there in the class, I went the lab and there she was experimenting on something I just looked at her and came back, I made sure she did not notice me .we started having our food together, after that camp we became much more closer and days passed by .

Two weeks before she had messaged me and sent me a wedding invitation and invited me for her wedding. I completely lost my control; I don't know what to do what can I say to her. how can she be so emotionless. but afterwards I realized that I was just thinking of only my side. I messaged her that can I come today. She replied to "me yeah sure please come". I packed my bag took the first bus I would and going to her.

He was crying when he was saying last few sentences, I understood his sincerity towards her ,its not easy for a man to love a same girl even after knowing he would never make her his own .i asked him his number and he gave me ,after listening to this story my respect towards him grew more. I reached my hometown I told him I have reached my stop but I my hearted says to travel with him and I had to go home. he said its fine, I can handle.

After some weeks I just ringed him to ask about what happened and how are you .when I called him for first time he did not pick my call, later he called me back ,I picked it up and asked what happened, He said nothing everything is fine. what about her, did you speak to her. Yeah, I spoke to her. He started telling me what happened.

I reached Mysore by 8 in the evening, I called her to ask about her exact location and she asked me to wait there and she would come to pick me up its only 2 days for her marriage.

After 15 minutes she came to pick me up. And I asked got down the car and looked at me and gave me a smile, and told me lets go, everyone is waiting there. I said okay .we reached her home, and her parents greeted me and some two person came and took my bag and said that they will take care of it, her father asked me to get in here sister brought me a cup of coffee and some sweets, and she was very silent she did not even speak a single word with even when we where way home. Her brother showed me my bedroom and got freshen up and after sometimes somebody knocked the door and opened it was her, come on let's have dinner. And she turned away, I pulled her hand inside and closed the door. She asked me what you are up to. Don't worry I am not going harm you, just need to talk to you, why are ignoring me like this I came here to see you to spend some time with you and you're just ignoring me like this, why? She burster into tears and sat in that bed. I totally got upset, I sat near to her took her hands and kept inside my palms ,why are you crying, sorry I was little upset after listening, to all these and when I came here, you are just ignoring me I was not able to bare that so I just busted on you sorry. She said its okay and I wiped her tears. Before coming to the camp my marriage was fixed and I was less bother about you, because I did not understand your pain and love towards me but when we again started talking and mingled with each other I came know how you loved me and how you care for me. Sometimes I thought I should say this to you and thinking that it may hurt you and I did not say that all I wanted you to be happy and make that camp a good memory of our life. And on that night when you where sitting near the pond, I came there to say that I am getting married and all you can do for me is to forget me and start a new life. But instead, when you kept your head on my shoulder, I felt to may this movement never end. After saying this she holds my hand and said if you love me so much please forget me and have a new journey. I wouldn't say anything even both my mind and heart gad no words to say. I was sad that she won't be mine and happy that she realized my love. She walked outside wiping her tears and eyes. I had no mood to have the dinner. I was still sitting there don't know what to do, I just wished if she told me this earlier or she would realize my love earlier. I was not able to do anything I was at a helpless condition. Next day when we went outside to pick our friends who had come to her marriage and we to pick them, on our way I asked, "Lana do you love me". It's too late now shahid. But tell me do you love me or not, she looked at me and said yes, I love you, that's all I wanted to hear from last 3 years and I asked her are you thinking what I am thinking, she looked at me and said don't even think of it, I will not be doing anything against my parents. We picked our friends and came back there is nothing left that I would do now. Next day I saw my Lana in the same way I saw in my dream but in my dream it was me and her, but here I had no role. I signaled her that you guys look great and already my heart broken into pieces, if I stand there for little more time the scene would get worsts, I went back her home took my bag and came from there. But I came to know that she loved me, and I will always love her.

While saying this voice was breaking and he hanged up the call. Without letting me speak anything. I called him back and his phone was switched off.

CAMP DAYS.

As MY wish it happend we both were on same team and thanks to **DR.muzamil** for makeing us in one team because he was leading the camp and he knew my whole story ,he came to me and this your last chance just make it work out because there only one year left ,he was my classmate and roommate and he was much worried about my smoking and I had promised him I would quit it soon and he create this chance so that I would quit. On Sunday evening we reached in that tribble village and it was a 10 days camp and we were staying in tent. A good Monday morning I woke early in the morning dressed up and went to the camp, I was the first person to reach there. I was already working on project ,that Muzammil had told me about a project that Safa was working which her father had assigned her to do for their hospital and she had promised him that she would do that ,but she was trying hard to finish it by time and she wouldn't do it ,so I thought I would do that for her and give her a surprise ,from last 3 days I was working on that ,even I have not worked so much hard for my own collage project . Has I reached earlier in camp I open my lap and started working on that ,I did not notice she had arrived there .she came and sat near me and asked me what are you doing .i said working on a project ,after few hours ,seeing my workload she asked me again that she can help me if i want ,but again I refused and said her to take rest .she opened her bag and took the water bottle ,it was so sunny day that my whole body was sweating ,she offered me a cup of cold water and said me drink the water and later work on the project .I looked at her and took water and started drinking it and her phone beeps and it was her dad ,she received it and moved from there ,after that she came to the camp and she started working on the same project that I was working for her ,she was been working it from past 10 days and today was the last date and she was not done with it yet . At last I finished that project. Her phone beeps again and it was her dad she answered it and she was saying that I almost finished it ,after hanging up she was murmuring herself and started working on it.I asked her whats the matter, why do you look so distrubed? she told me she had a projected and had finish it by today and she was not done yet and dad started asking about it. Shah called her for some work and she went with him. I had finished the whole project and checked it again already crowd had been coming for the camp. I created a fake email and mailed her. She came back and open her laptop and saw a notification ,she opened it and it was her project from and it was from an unknown mail ,she was shocked and was very happy for it and called Muzammil asking that have he sent any mail he said that he have not sent anything .she was in a happy mood and sent that mail to her dad and called him ."*I have sent it just check it and say me whether is it okay or should I change anything* " and hanged her phone .she was talking like the whole project was her own idea .I was just looking at the patients but my whole concentration has on her .she came near me stared helping me with my work ,I asked her what happened you are in good mood .yeah! didn't I tell you about the work I completed it and sent it to my dad and he was so happy with it ,thank god ,she told turned towards the patients I asked her you told me that It wasn't over yet , no I just finished it .Me who knows the whole truth about that project and first of all it was me one who done the whole project and she did not reveal the truth. later it was evening we finished the camp and headed back to our tents .i was so tiered that I would go sleep on busy street .but I had promised Mohith and nishmal that we would vist the village ,I took a bath from the near by pond and dressed up and went outside .I was fond the village atmosphere and that climate. I open my phone I had 2 missed call from my mother .I called her back ,these mothers are so different from whole world because they how much you growup older you are still small child for them and they take care of each and everything and their children are only their priority even he or she is married they don't allow anyone in their position and noone can fill their place . she picked up the call and asked me about what you are doing, how are you, did you have coffee and how is the climate there, did you apply the oil on your hair etc....... she asked everything and told me go to bed fast and hanged up. I came near tea stall and ordered a tea and brought a cigarette and I lighted and waited for both of them to com. I was smoking and drinking the tea." hey shahid " I hear a voice I looked around and I did not find any one ,later someone tapped me from behind ,when turned back it was her safa, the smoke inside my mouth came out and started coughing ,she moved back because of that smoke and started scolding me .

Lana - “from when did this habit came to you, why do you pay money to die, give that some poor that may give some good deeds ”,

listening that I throwed that cigarette, it was my first time I threw the cigarette without finishing it ,it was only because she had been there and I don’t want to create a bad impression ,

Shahid- ”sorry ,madam .yeah tell me why did you come to see me ”.

she sat near me

Safa- “I had been to Muzammil ,tell me the truth was it you who sent me the mail ”,

I nodded and said

Shahid- “no it wasn’t me and what is this mail about”,

she stared at me. she had been to Muzammil and told about the unknown mail and how much happy her father was and he was very proud of her. After listening this Muzammil had told the truth about the unknown mail and he told her that I was working on it day and night, and he still loves you.

Safa- “don’t act to much, tell me the truth or else wait let me call Muzammil”.

Shahid- “no that’s fine, yeah it was me, Muzammil had told about your project and you not able complete it ,so I thought I could help you"

Safa-" okay and why didn't you tell me about it, In the morning"

Shahid- "did'nt you tell that you don't like owing things from others so ,I did not mention you about it "

mohith and nishmal had reached there and told me tells go.I asked her do you want to join,she told that she have work left. and was leaving from there.

safa- "by the way thanks"

Shahid – "your welcome"

Safa – "don't start smoking again, I am leaving"

Shahid – "don't leave, always be with me than I won't smoke again"

Looking at me and laughing she nodded and headed back to her tent. i was just laughing by thinking her words and happier that she cares about me. I think I got my old safa back even though she knows that I love her. After we took a whole round in that village and had our dinner I went back to the tent, I had a good sleep. I got up late that day and already everyone had been there at work. she had been there before I reach there, she was looking more beautiful than before, I don't know is it because my love towards her had grown more or she is always like that. she waved at me, and we stared helping each other we enjoyed our camp ,it was time for lunch and I just called her that lets have the lunch together and she said okay fine then let's go , we went an hotel inside that village and had the lunch there it was very wonderful to spend time with her ,her voice and her naughty attitude and always that pointed nose that was the first thing I noticed ,when she came into the class at the beginning, later having the lunch we moved into the camp one way she asked me do you still love me ,I did not reply anything.

Okay fine don't tell me.my inner voice was shouting like "how can I tell you, how much I love you, don't act has a fool, after knowing everything" but my voice did not come out, we just walked silently. Days passed so fast, and with this camp I got my safa back with this camp. we used to go have the food together, visiting the village . One day while crossing the road she holds my hands and l looked at her, but she wasn't looking at me, I started shivering with fear. We almost walked miles together holding our hands, finally we reached back to our tents it was last day of our camp she looked at me, we both met with an eye contact and stayed a long time like that. all she wanted to say was in her eye and I think she really loved me, but she never told me that she loved me. later that night I lost my whole sleep I was just thinking of that, my eyes started rolling the tears, I would not control my emotions, I started crying like child. I was not able to sleep that whole night, next day morning she came in search of, it was an early morning I was near the lake side, I was so sleepy, and she came near me and asked me why you are standing here, I said, just like that enjoying the view. why are you eye red did you smoke again? she asked me. no did not; I did not sleep the whole night. I thought she would ask me why? but she did not because, she knew the reason. we sat there for long time, slowly she kept her head on my shoulder ,I did not react for it instead I made it more comfortable for her to lay down. After an hour her phone rang and it was her friend and she had to go, she asked me when are you leaving I said later . I was not ready to leave that place because that place had given me more memories of her, that's the place where spent our most important part of my life ,and that place will always be special one for me . she packed her bag and everyone started moving into the bus I had already packed my bag ,I went to bus at sat near the window .Muzammil who saw me gave me a smile like he couldn't help me more than this .and I was very thankful for him. That day at night we reached back to our hostel. I slept as I went into the bed .After two days of rest and holiday we came back to class and I was looking for her, she was not there in the class, I went the lab and there she was experimenting on something I just looked at her and came back, I made sure she did not notice me .we started having our food together, after that camp we became much more closer and days passed by .

later he had a study holidays and one day she had messaged me and sent me a wedding invitation and invited me for her wedding. I completely lost my control; I don't know what to do what can I say to her. how can she be so emotionless. but afterwards I realized that I was just thinking of only my side. After thinking it for days, I messaged her that can I come today. She replied to me" yeah sure, please come". I packed my bag took the first bus I would and going to her.

He was crying when he was saying last few sentences, I understood his sincerity towards her ,its not easy for a man to love a same girl even after knowing he would never make her his own .I asked him his number and he gave me ,after listening to this story my respect towards him grew more. I reached my hometown I told him I have reached my stop but I my hearted says to travel with him and I had to go home. he said its fine, I can handle.

HIS CALL.

After some weeks I just ringed him to ask about what happened and how are you .when I called him for first time he did not pick my call, later he called me back ,I picked it up and asked what happened, He said nothing everything is fine. what about her, did you speak to her. Yeah, I spoke to her. He started telling me what happened.

I reached Mysore by 8 in the evening, I called her to ask about her exact location and she asked me to wait there and she would come to pick me up its only 2 days for her marriage.

After 15 minutes she came to pick me up. And got down the car and looked at me and gave me a smile, and told me lets go, everyone is waiting there. I said okay . On the way we both had somuch to talk, but neither of us were ready to put out our feelings, we reached her home, the whole place was looking like a palace, decorated wiith lights and flowers and her parents greeted me and some two person came and took my bag and said that they will take care of it everyone ther was busy with the wedding work , her father asked me how was the journey and started talking about the marriage ,meanwhile her sister brought me a cup of coffee and some sweets, and she was very silent she did not even speak a single word. Her brother showed me my bedroom and got freshen up and after sometimes somebody knocked the door and opened it was her, come on let's have dinner and she went of, I went down to have the Dinner, whole family was present in front the table and everyone was waiting for me,I was like just standup and shout out that I love her and I don't want loos her, It creat huge mess and frankly I was bold enough .later after the dinner I came back to my room, she entered to my room with a jar full of water and a cup.I asked how are you ,when I asked her this, she sat on the bed and started crying, I went to her and asked "hey what happend, why are crying "I took her hand kept inside my both hands and started rubbing it softly to make her comfortable. She told me "how can I be so emotionless and how much more will I ingnore you, I thought you would get anger on me".I said "Its okay, and wiped her tears " but inside me I am dieing with pain and I dont want to show it to her.Its already late for me react.

she started speaking, Before coming to the camp my marriage was fixed and I was less bother about you, because I did not understand your pain and love towards me but when we again started talking and mingled with each other I came know how you loved me and how you care for me. Sometimes I thought I should say this to you and thinking that it may hurt you and I did not say that all I wanted you to be happy and make that camp a good memory of our life. And on that morning ,when you where sitting near the pond, I came there to say that I am getting married and all you can do for me is to forget me and start a new life. But instead, when I saw your face, I just kept my head on your shoulder, I felt that may this movement never end. After saying this she holds my hand and said if you love me so much please forget me and have a new journey. I wouldn't say anything even both my mind and heart had no words to say. I was sad that she won't be mine and happy that she realized my love. She walked outside wiping her tears and eyes. I was still sitting there don't know what to do, I just wished if she told me this earlier or she would realize my love earlier. I was not able to do anything I was at a helpless condition. Next day when we went outside to pick our friends who had come to her marriage and we to pick them, on our way I asked, "Safa do you love me". It's too late now shahid. But tell me do you love me or not, she looked at me and said "yes, I love you", that's all I wanted to hear from last 4 years and I asked her are you thinking what I am thinking, she looked at me and said don't even think of it, I will not be doing anything against my parents. We picked our friends and came back there is nothing left that I would do now. Next day I saw my Safa in the same way I saw in my dream but in my dream it was me and her, but here I had no role. I signaled her that you guys look great and already my heart broken into pieces, if I stand there for little more time the scene would get worsts, I went back her home took my bag and came from there. But I came to know that she loved me, and I will always love her.

While saying this voice was breaking and he hanged up the call. Without letting me speak anything. I called him back and his phone was switched off.

2 YEARS LATER

After two years, while I was scrolling my contact list and I saw his number, I called him the phone was ringing and he picked it up and asked I asked him how are you? And he said where the hell were you been these long time ,and I asked him where are you. and what are you doing, he said that, he finished his graduation and now he have an small clinic in that Trible village where he had been for the camp, to always make her memories a pleasant one and to feel that she is always with me. In this village. I used to go near the pond every evening where we both have sat together, and our heart spoke loveder than our lips. I asked him that still you haven't come out of it. he laughed and said I don't think so I can. I asked him that did you ever meet her again after that."no I have not, she had called me after that many times but I didnot pick up ".

"shahid are you happy now",if" I yes thats true in one way, and If I say no thats to true farhan".

I wish she would been yours. he laughes and tells me "even it was my wish from last 6 years, but god have decided something and now I am happy with this life in this life brother."shahid we should meet. "yeah sure come the village I just whatsapp you the place".

we hanged our call.

the end.

TO YOU.

I wrote this story. in belive that you would read this and to those love birds and lovers,I have an message we are not born in this world for one person. But when we are failed in love we are not a failure in our life, instead we learn many things to start a new life. A new journey is always waiting us. even they both are separated they both are their own new life.

> "*tell them and realize others, love before its too late, sometimes you would wish them to come to your life onces again and it will be to late for you to rewind the past.*"

9 798888 150146

Printed by Libri Plureos GmbH in Hamburg,
Germany